Never Make an Uninformed Financial Decision Again

Book 2 - Starting to Make Money

by Hayden Burrus

Table of Contents

Chapter 1 -- How to Get More Money

Getting more money is a topic that most finance books don't cover. Financial advisers seem to focus on how to use your current financial portfolio to improve your financial quality of life down the road. They don't do much to help you figure out how to convert your hard work and abilities into a financial portfolio in the first place. For most people younger than retirement age, achieving success in getting money is the most critical component in securing a financial future.

The median annual household income in the US is a little over $50K per year. If an "average" household can figure out how to get $60K next year instead of $50K, this household's financial portfolio is improved by $10K next year. If that same household has a financial portfolio of $50,000, it would have to figure out how to improve its investment return by 20% after investment fees ($50,000 x 20% = $10K). No financial advisor is going to claim he can beat the market by 20% plus expenses. So, until you've amassed a six- or seven- digit financial portfolio, increasing your earnings is your more powerful path to improving your financial portfolio.

Numerous studies show that there is a strong correlation between education level and household income. So improving your education level is a strong path to increasing income. Now, I appreciate that many people are not in a position to quit their jobs and go back to school and get a degree. Well, getting a degree is only one way to increase your educational level (and one of the hardest at that). Your educational level and ability to earn more money increases whenever you gain any skill that is valuable to your employer and/or clients. You can even focus on skills that are valuable to employers that you hope will hire you in the future.

So, the first step down the road of getting more money is determining a new skill that is valuable to your employer. Look around at the other people working at your company. Identify someone who makes a little more than you do. Then determine what education or skill they have that you don't. Maybe they have an advanced technical skill, maybe that person supervises people, and maybe that person manages budgets or sells to prospects. The list goes on. Now acquire those skills that you are missing.

Most of the education you need for the next step in your career won't be from formal certification or class work. Instead, it will be informally developed through reading, guidance from someone who already has the skill you want, and hands-on practice.

Let's go through some examples. If you want to acquire the skill of managing project budgets, you need both knowledge as well as practice. Your local library will have books on the topic. Get one and read it. Also, find a task that you can take on that requires you to manage budgets. For example, offer to organize the company Christmas party. Prepare a budget; share it with your bosses and anyone else that needs to fund your budget. Offer to help out on any of the budgeting tasks at your company; don't expect to get paid for this help, you are delivering the help for the experience.

Another skill that can help many people increase their value is the skill of supervising people effectively. Again, there are lots of books on this in the local library. Get one and read it. Get some supervisory experience by taking on something at your job. Offer to train the new people. If there are no obvious ways to get supervisory experience where you work, you can do it in your free time. Lead your kids' Cub Scout Troop, join a local club and be visible by leading a fundraiser (and make sure your bosses know about it), join the local Chamber of Commerce and be a visible part of their committees. Then demonstrate these skills on the job. You won't get paid for this extra work, but you will be in a better position to get a promotion down the line. Other employers will take notice as well.

What if you have a dead end job or your boss hates you and there is just no way you're ever going to get a raise? Yes, that's possible. The process is the same as what I outlined above, except in that case, you should work on getting your raise from your next employer.

You have a clear path to acquire any skill that separates you from a higher income. Take it! Then you've got your higher income and you'll have improved your financial portfolio by far more than any financial advisor possibly could have done for you.

Chapter 2 -- Spending or Saving

Spending and saving are two sides of the same coin. Every spending decision you make can be reinterpreted as a saving decision. When you spend money, you are deciding not to save. When you save money, you are deciding not to spend. Definitely keep that in mind when you are deciding how to spend your money. Yes, you are going to spend it. One of the things that you can spend money on is your savings! Doesn't that sound awesome? You'll have so much fun enjoying your savings. Ok, I appreciate that not many people get excited when thinking about spending their hard- earned money on savings, but they should. I get excited about saving money. When I am able to save more because of an increase in income or a reduction in expenses, it makes me happy. Let me share why.

Every dollar I have saved makes a future purchase that much closer. In addition, a saved dollar makes a future unexpected expense that much less fearful. A saved dollar also might be invested so that it can increase my income and spending in the future. Finally, a saved dollar delivers a safety net to allow me to take a risk to try something new in life. So a saved dollar can deliver a lot of happiness, certainly a lot more happiness than any purchase I walked away from when I chose to save my dollar.

Think of a really fun two week vacation. If you are single, that might set you back $2,000. A Thursday night out with your friends can set you back $100. So next Thursday, if you decide to stay home, think of your decision as getting a step closer to a vacation that you are going to enjoy and spend the rest of your life remembering. Saving money helps you deliver future happiness.

Now the other side of the coin: Think of a disaster that might come your way some day-- maybe a stolen car, or getting fired. That stings. It's not fun. You're upset. Now you have to figure out how to come up with the money to get you through this disaster. You need a new car; or you need spending money to hold you over until you get your next job. If you've saved your money, that problem is solved easily. Just go to your savings account and take out the money you need to fix the problem. If the savings account isn't there for you, you get hit again. You are going to have to go to credit cards (and feel the pain of stupidity), or even worse, friends and family (and feel the pain of humiliation) to get the money. In a time of disaster, the last thing you'll need is an additional source of pain. Skipping a few Thursday nights out will provide you with an emergency fund to help you avoid this financial pain.

After you have your emergency fund in place, you must explore investing some of your savings. Investing is the most fun of all. You get to make your money work for you. Over the long-term, the stock market doubles about once every seven years. Invest your savings; let it ride for seven years. Your investment gains are now equal to your savings and can be returned to you as free money. Go out and spend it if there is something you need. Your original investment is still left untouched and will still return more investment income to you in future years. This is awesome. Investing is fun. Now you may feel that seven years is a long time to wait for your money, but most of us will still be interested in spending money in seven years. The money you spend then might as well be free money from investment gains. Everyone agrees that free money is much more fun to spend than your own money.

But wait! There's more! You may have so much fun investing that once seven years is complete, you'll want to invest again and double your money again. If you can be patient, your money will balloon in size:

Number of Years	Number of Doubles	Value of $10,000 Investment
0	0	10,000
7	1	20,000
14	2	40,000
21	3	80,000
28	4	160,000
35	5	320,000
42	6	640,000
49	7	1,280,000
56	8	2,560,000
63	9	5,120,000
70	10	10,240,000

While almost nobody has a 70-year time horizon, most people still do have enough time to enjoy the financial security that several investment doubles provide.

At some points in your life, you will want to live out your dreams and try something new but will be concerned with how your cash flow will be affected. Let your savings come to save the day! Dream of quitting, hate your boss, but don't know where to get your next paycheck? Let your savings allow you to fulfill your dreams. Maybe you want to open up a flower shop but you don't know where you'll get the money. Let your savings save the day and fulfill your dreams.

Saving money isn't about sacrificing your fun today in order to be a responsible person. That's boring. Saving money is about avoiding the pains that life can deliver to you, and at the same time delivering life-long memories and fulfilling your dreams. Saving money is about the most fun a person can have.

Chapter 3 -- What Would You Do With $1000?

Let's continue our fun thought experiment from earlier, except now you are getting $1000. That's a lot better than $100 and it can be more than a night out. You'll still have to show up at work tomorrow. Dare I say that you should save this money, too? If you can put yourself $1000 ahead, you can pay for a tune up to your car and help extend the life of your car for a few years. You can pay down your credit card bill and avoid the exorbitant 29% annual interest charge they are ramming down your throat. Right there, you are saving another $24.17 each month in interest charges ($24.17 / month x 12 months = $290.00 / year = 29% of $1000). There are lots of things you can do with $1000.

Maybe you can get ahead on some of your bills; maybe you can prepay your car insurance bill and avoid finance charges. Maybe you can use the $1000 to push your bank balance high enough where you no longer have to pay the maintenance fee because your bank account is below the minimum balance. As an aside, when I was a kid, I asked my mom, "Why are they charging an account maintenance fee to the people with the smallest bank balances? They clearly need the bank account the least and also can't afford it." Her answer: "Because they can." I went to the bank and closed my bank account.

My point with these thought exercises is this: You should think about how you will handle unexpected windfalls. These things do happen in life. If you've already made plans to save a windfall, you will be less likely to do something impulsive and wasteful with the money.

How about investing? Some people may suggest you use the $1000 to start investing. I disagree. It's still too soon. Many mutual funds have minimum opening balances. Brokerage accounts often don't, but the expenses associated with buying a stock are quite expensive relative to the $1000 investment. These expenses effectively lower your return. First you have a broker's commission. At online brokers that will be around $10, or 1% of your investment. Count on another 1% commission expense when you sell.

Next you have the bid/ask spread. The bid/ask spread is the difference between the highest price someone is willing to buy the stock (the bid price) and the lowest price at which someone is willing to sell the stock (the ask price). When you are buying a stock, you have to pay the higher "ask" price. Then the stock has to increase in value just for the bid price to rise up to the price you paid for the stock. For heavily traded stocks, the bid/ask spread is not significant. However for micro-cap stocks and penny stocks (stocks that trade for less than $1 per share) the bid/ask spread can be a few percentage points.

Finally you have the issue of volatility. At this level, this isn't a financial cost. Volatility is more of a psychological cost. The price swings in a one stock investment are a lot greater than the price swings of the stock market as a whole. If you turn on the Business Channel, you'll hear a stock profile every day of a stock that went up or down 50% in the past few months. If you make the effort to follow those stocks for another few months, you might notice it having a price swing just as large in the opposite direction. Watching the value of your $1000 investment go to $1500 one month and then $750 the next month can be stressful. That stress may make you shyer about investing in the future when you have more money. You definitely don't want that. There's a time to begin investing. The time is not when you get your first $1,000.

Chapter 4 -- First Investments - It's not Just for Stocks

The most common entry point for retirement investing is stocks -- either through a mutual fund, or through direct purchase of shares. Usually these purchases are made as a result of opening an IRA or 401(k) account. Stocks and the stock market are great first investments -- they are easy to understand, easy to buy and sell, and can have low investment expenses. However, stocks aren't the only things out there for which you can use your first investment dollars for.

It goes without saying, but I am going to say it anyway -- building a solid emergency fund must be a higher priority than investing. The savings you will reap personally and financially from an emergency fund in times of trouble will be far larger than the returns generated if the emergency fund were invested instead. Go ahead and read Chapter 10 in Book 1 ("Emergency Fund - What's the Point?") again if you forgot this important point.

OK, so you have your emergency fund set and even a little extra. You are ready to begin investing. First off, if you have an employer that will match your contributions to a 401(k), then do that. Your employer's match is free money and free money is the best kind of money. Many employers offer a 50% match up to 6% of your income contributed to your 401(k). If your employer does that, then your employer will deposit $500 into your retirement account for every $1,000 you put in. $500 in free money! A guaranteed 50% return on your retirement investment! Take it!

If your employer does not offer a company match to your 401(k) or you have extra money for investing after your 401(k) contribution, read on. Think about investing in yourself and your household. Keep in mind I used the word "investing" and not spending. Buying a new Cadillac is probably not an investment in yourself. If you are an Uber driver and a new Cadillac will help you make more money, then the Cadillac could be considered an investment. But if your new car won't help you increase your income or reduce your spending, it isn't an investment.

Investing in yourself and your family is the best investment you can make. Payoffs can be financial and personal. So what does an investment in yourself look like? An investment in yourself increases your income and/or happiness at some future point. Think of someone who does what you do but makes more money than you. What is it about them that allow them to make more money? Do they have a degree or certificate that you don't have? Maybe you should invest your extra money (and time) in obtaining that degree.

Maybe you have a side business that could benefit from advertising, or more effort from you in growing the business. You could cut back on your hours at your job and invest your money in paying your living expenses for a few months while you get your side business off the ground.

There might be a higher paying job that you've always wanted to do but are currently unqualified for. Spend some time researching that job. Find out what qualifications you need to get in the door. Find out how long it will take once you get in to pass your current income. Then put a price tag on each of the steps. You can invest your money (and time) toward that goal.

First investments can also work on the other side of wealth creation. A first investment can reduce your expenses. Eliminating debt is the obvious choice. Paying off debt eliminates interest payments, delivering more wealth to you. Related to eliminating debt is eliminating payment plans. Most payment plans have some sort of service charge, and many companies offer a "full payment discount." If you have the money, the savings from a full payment discount is a bonus.

When you look at your budget, if you see regular expenses for renting or leasing things (e.g. cars, tools, furniture), consider whether you would be better off if you bought the item outright and got rid of all your future rental fees.

Once you are ready to make your first investments, you may not have to look any further than the mirror. If you are not going to invest in yourself and your life, nobody will.

Chapter 5 -- Time is Money

Ben Franklin popularized this formula. We've all said it, heard it and used it. The web, which seems to have an answer for everything, can't completely decide what it means. There are dozens of sites that ask the question and each comes up with a slightly different answer. The Cambridge Dictionary says it "... emphasizes that you should not waste time, because you could be using it to earn money." I agree, but I think it refers to an even deeper relationship to the two. It's kind of like "Clicks are customers" for web businesses, or miles and minutes being equivalent for runners.

The key point here is that you can compare and translate units of time into money and vice versa. The most common translation is when you think of your value at work in a dollars per hour fashion. When you have a fixed conversion rate you can make work decisions based on a which is worth more basis: the dollars you get for working or the free hours you get by not working. That much is straightforward -- it's "Time is Money 101." We can amp up your use of this personal finance equation and use it more often and more thoughtfully.

When should you use the T=M equation? Always. If the rip-off gas station close to your house charges $0.25 more per gallon than the one next to Wal-Mart 10 miles away, it may bug you, but if things are going well with your money, it's not worth it to spend the extra 15 minutes of time in the car driving to Wal-Mart just for gas. Your 15 minutes of free time will be worth more than the $3 or $4 you'll save at Wal-Mart on a fill up. What if you are really tight on cash right now? Then the value of money is higher right now. In that case, maybe you should drive to Wal-Mart. What if you've got nothing to do on a Saturday afternoon? Then the value of your free time is lower. What if you have more money than you need to spend? Then the value of the $3 savings at Wal-Mart is very low to you. Lastly, you could get your teenager to do it. Teenagers have lots of excess free time, so their free time is worth a lot less than yours.

The above example brings out a lot of nuances in the T=M equation. First, you can use it all the time, not just at work. Second, your conversion rate between time and money will change depending on what is going on in your life. Third, the relationship between time and money for you will be different than its relationship for me or anyone else. Fourth, you'll notice that your income, even expressed in a dollars per hour fashion, doesn't have a direct relationship to the T=M equation unless you are at work.

Here's another one I encountered when I first started letting the T=M equation guide my life. I was at the airport and didn't want to be bored on the plane. So I decided to get some reading material at the gift shop. I gravitated over to the magazine section because that is what you are supposed to do before you get on the plane. But hey! I noticed the magazine costs five dollars and I figured that I would probably be done with it by the time the plane lands in 90 minutes. A book costs $19 and will likely give me ten hours of reading time, including both my outbound and return flight. Yes, the book costs four times more but gives me almost seven times the reading pleasure. It's a no brainer! The interesting thing here is the fact that airport books are overpriced is irrelevant. Yes, I could (and should) have gone to the library and saved the money I spent buying airport reading material. But at the airport before a flight the free library book is no longer possible. At the airport, my best choice is to put the magazine down and buy the book.

Here's the most fun example. Depending on where you live, a week at Disneyworld for your family may run you two to three thousand dollars. Wow! A week at a nearby beach town may run you one thousand. Your family will definitely have fun at both places. On the surface the choice is obvious; you are going to the beach. You can have your week of fun and save a thousand dollars at the beach. You've gone to the beach every year for the past five years and you know it's fun. It's a sure thing. But here's the thing about the value of experiences as opposed to the value of things. With experiences, you have to count the fun you have during the experience (one week) and the fun you have remembering the experience. If your family has never been to Disney World before and wants to go, the trip will likely generate lots of memories. Each time you spend five minutes happily reminiscing about your trip, those five minutes should be added to the one week of happiness at Disneyworld. More likely than not, you will reminisce more about your one trip to Disneyworld than your sixth vacation at the beach. Are the extra memories worth the extra $1000 you will be paying for the trip? That's hard to tell. But let me give you a start in figuring that out. A five minute memory relived once a week for the next forty years is 173 hours of happiness. If all four people in your family experience another 173 hours of happy memories in their lives, that's 692 total hours of happy memories for the additional money you spent on the Disney trip.

One more. You have a one hour commute through rush hour traffic. You hate it. You could avoid the commute by moving closer to work, which will cost you $500 more per month in rent. Is it worth it to move? Well, moving might save you 45 minutes off your one hour commute, each way, every day (20 work days times two commutes per day times 45 minutes of unpleasantness avoided equals 30 hours of unpleasantness avoided per month). Reducing your commute will also save you money each month on gas ($100) and car maintenance ($100).

So, here your decision boils down to 30 hours of unpleasantness if you don't move or $300 extra expense ($500 rent increase minus $200 savings on commuting). That one might go either way. Are you willing to pay $10 per hour to convert your commute into leisure time?

One last interesting thing here is that although your commute is an experience just like your trip to Disney World, it is a negative experience, so it should be treated differently. Generally people who have a positive disposition don't waste any time rehashing negative experiences. You probably won't spend five minutes a week remembering bumper-to-bumper traffic. So the time value of memories of negative experiences is zero.

In this chapter, I gave four real-world examples on how to use T=M in everyday life. One global takeaway from all these examples is that the notion of "time" in the equation takes on a slightly different meaning in each example. First, I start with the traditional value of work time; then about valuing free time, reading time (or maybe about non-boredom), happy time, and lastly about avoiding unpleasant time. Each of these types of time has a different relationship to money.

If you are like me, you'll find that using T=M in your decision-making will not only be fun, but it will increasingly give you the confidence that you are making the right decision. Of course you'll also find that after a few smart applications of T=M in your life, you'll have more time and more money. Thanks, Ben Franklin.

Chapter 6 -- Skip the Car Loan and Pay Cash

Avoiding the car loan is the single most important far-reaching personal finance decision that can be made in your life. If I were to determine if a young adult was on the road to financial independence and I could ask that person only one question, my question would be "Have you ever had a car loan?" The correct answer is "No." If you have to answer "yes" to that question, at least add "...but never again..." to your answer.

When a person signs her name on the bottom line of a car loan promissory note, she is agreeing to do more than pay back the car loan. A person who gets a car loan must do all of the following: 1) pay $5,260 in interest charges (assuming a eight year 5.0% loan); 2) pay "origination fees" (origination fees can be a few hundred dollars); 3) pay late fees if you ever forget to pay on time (you will); 4) buy comprehensive and collision insurance. Yeah, "comp and collision" is usually required on a car loan. It's not necessary on a junky car, so this is a waste of money for you. Once you are "all in," you will end up paying about $32K that you currently don't have just to get a $25K car that you just have to have right now. Now tell me that you would be able to sleep well at night knowing that.

"That's easy for you to say. I'm only 22 years old and I don't have 25 grand lying around to buy a car." Ah yes, I've heard that before. People love to apply the false premise that they have to buy a car right now and all cars cost the same as the car that you want to buy right now. Buy a $2000 jalopy. Take the bus. Walk. Rent a car when you need it. In the meanwhile save your money.

"But I'm just starting out; I don't have anything left over at the end of the month. I can't save money!" OK, Mr. Irrational. You have no car and you can't save money. How exactly, Mr. Irrational, were you expecting to afford your car payment, insurance payment, gas money, and inevitable car maintenance costs? It's time to tighten your belt. You better save some money. If you have a job and no car, you should be able to find a way to save a few hundred dollars per month.

Now, let's fast forward three or four months down the road. With your disciplined budgeting, you should have about $1000 in the bank but no car. Now go ahead and open up Craigslist, or whatever used car classifieds are in your area. Find the cars that cost less than the amount you have in the bank and go shopping. In a few days you should be driving home in a ~~shiny new~~ car. In fact, this car will probably be old and crappy. It will have more than its fair share of repairs and it won't last very long. Maybe only one or two years. But it's yours, and you don't have a car payment, hooray!

Let's fast forward some more. Say a year and a half. Your first car has turned to junk. You are still a disciplined spender. You've put up $100 a month or so for repairs and maintenance. You've continued to save about $200 a month even while owning your first car. Guess what! Without even looking you have about $3600 in the bank (18 months times $200 equals $3600). You call the "we buy junk cars" telephone number you saw on the side of the road. The junk guy offers you $400 for your junk car (that's about the going rate nowadays). Now you've got $4000 to spend on your next car.

$4000 won't buy you a new car, but it will buy you a reliable five to seven year old small car. This car can last you ten more years if you take care of it. All the while you are still saving your $200 per month. You might even be able to save $300 per month because this one won't have as high a repair cost.

Let's fast forward ten years. You saved about $250 a month for ten years. Guess what? Now you've got $30,000 plus a little interest in the bank waiting for you to buy your next car. The world is your oyster. Any car that goes for $30K new, you'll be able to get for $21K if you accept a model one or two years old. Do that, you'll still have a nice car and you'll be able to put $10K in an emergency fund as well.

Keep saving (probably about $300 or $400 a month because you won't have any maintenance costs for the first few years). In a few more years you'll have the money for your next car ready to go. Your savings after that point can be invested. You're heading down the road to be the millionaire next door.

You're welcome. You just got a road map to transform yourself from a person destined to spend his entire life being a slave to car payments and at risk of having your car repossessed to a guy who strolls into a car dealership, says "I'll take that one," hands over a check, and walks out the door. And it isn't even hard. How awesome.

So now that the issue of "how can I possibly skip car loans?" has been put to rest, I want to tackle the issue of "Why bother skipping car loans?"

Mr. Wateawile, who follows the game plan above, is going to be debt-free investor, have a late model car, and a decent sized emergency fund in eleven years or so.

His friend, Ms. Havitnou, decides to get the $25K car right away and signs on the dotted line for a shiny new car, car loan, interest payments, and origination fees. Her new car sure has a lot of add-ons. Five, no, eight, years down the road her loan is paid off.

You see, if Ms. Havitnou asks for a five year car loan, she'll have to pay $470/month which is too much for her to afford; she has to get the eight year loan so her payment can go down to $315/month; she has the ability to spend about $300/month on her car, just like Wateawile. Eight years down the road, Havitnou has no car loan, and no savings. She's about $1,500 in debt because she had to pay the origination fees and insurance that Wateawhile avoided. She sees Wateawile's car and gets jealous. She just has to have a new one. She walks into the dealership and asks to trade in her eight year old car and get a new car. The dealer offers $6,500 for her trade which she gladly accepts. She uses $1,500 to pay off her debts and puts $5,000 towards her new car. She gets another 8 year car loan and walks out the door. She's hooked on car loans and doesn't even know it.

Not far into their adult lives, the two friends are on very different paths. Wateawile is debt-free and saving money; Havitnou is on a never ending cycle of car loan debt. She's one missed payment from getting her car repossessed and not having a car at all. Eventually an unexpected financial disaster strikes-- everyone has a few in their lives and they are always at the worst time. Havitnou misses her car payment. The repo man comes out and takes the car away, and Havitnou is taking the bus. She looks out the bus window and sees Wateawile driving to work in his car with a smile on his face. Wateawile is smiling because he is thinking about his flush savings account. Wateawile notices Havitnou on the bus deep in thought and wonders how things turned out so differently for the two of them.

Chapter 7 -- Spend Less Than You Earn (Except When You Don't)

The best part about this financial advice is that it applies to everyone in the world regardless of life situation, age, or income level. My son gets $6 a week in allowance. If he tries to spend $7, or even $6, he's not going to have enough money for when he needs to buy a big ticket item (say $20). If you make $500 / week, you better not spend it all, or one day when you have unexpected expenses, you won't be able to pay them. That's true for $5000 / week or even $50,000 / week. Spending less than you earn is always possible, no matter how little you earn. It involves sacrifice, but it's possible. Spending less than you earn leads to some great things like an emergency fund, peace of mind, the ability to make less stressed short-term decisions, and ultimately the ability to invest in your future. We've beaten that part to death in other parts of this book.

What about the 2nd part of the chapter title? Yup, I am a financial coach that gives you permission to spend more than you earn in a few select instances. Let's start with a quiz: Is it OK to spend more than you earn when 1) you have an unexpected $1000 car repair; or 2) you have an unexpected $1000 emergency room visit; or 3) your mom unexpectedly asks you for $1000 because she lost her job. Yes it is OK in all cases. The key here is that all of these situations are unexpected and are not part of your day to day (or even month to month) budget.

I am giving you permission to open up your savings account, transfer money to checking, and write a $1000 check to get out of your "unexpected" financial predicament. Whaa? You don't have a savings account; no money under the mattress? Now you're in a real bind.

No, don't even think about using that IRA. That's for retirement. You said so when you put the money in. That's the worst source of cash for your predicament. When you take money from your IRA to get yourself out of the mess you are in, the government is the most usurious lender. The government will charge you 35% interest <u>per second</u> to take money out of your IRA!!! Actually, it's 35%[1] per second for the first second. After that your interest cost is the investment return you would have gotten if you left the money in your IRA to begin with.

Before you begin to toy with drawing money from the IRA, imagine your withdrawal scenario all the way through to the end. You go to your friendly IRA custodian (e.g. Vanguard, Fidelity, etc.) and say "I'm

---

1 It will be 35% if you are in the 25% tax bracket and you don't pay state income tax (25% + 10% early withdrawal penalty). A single person making $50K per year in the state of Texas will fall into this category. The cost to withdraw could be as low as 10% or well over 50% depending on your income and state of residence.

in a bind; I need to take out $1000 from my IRA now instead of when I retire. Can you help?"

"Sure," the account representative says," but you'll need to take a little more out for taxes."

"OK, I guess I'll have to," you say. "I really need the money now." You hold out your hand, and the account rep pulls out a stack of $100s. When the first one lands in your hand, you are already starting to feel like your problems are melting away.

"Onetwothreefour fivesixseveneightnineten eleventwelvethirteenfourteenfifteen." The account rep takes a deep breath. "Here's $1500 from your IRA. On your next IRA statement, you'll see a $1500[2] withdrawal and your total balance will be $1500 lower than yesterday plus or minus investment returns. That should take care of your problem."

"Thanks," you respond not knowing what else to say.

"Now walk with me," the rep says. You absent mindedly follow him with the 15 Ben Franklins still in your hand. "Open your hand."

"Whaa?" You look up and realize that he took you to a toilet.

-----

[2] I rounded this number for dramatic effect. The math nerds will tell you that the real IRA withdrawal requirement is $1,538.46; $538.46 is 35% of $1,538.46 leaving you with $1000.

"Onetwothreefourfive." The account rep is taking bills from your hand. He throws them into the toilet shuts the lid and flushes. You notice that on the toilet lid the initials "I.R.S." "Have a nice day!" the account rep calls out as you walk out of the office building in a daze. You weren't even back at your car before you realized you made a bad choice.

In other words, don't take money from your IRA.

Your best bet after savings is getting a line of credit on your home or some other item you have of value. But if you have no savings, you probably have no home equity either, so I am not going to spend any time on that option.

If you don't have money under the mattress, your best option if available is to borrow, not withdraw, money from your 401(k). You can do this in some cases (such as medical costs). Your 401(k) will put you on a strict repayment plan, with interest. But at least there is no penalty and the interest is going right back into your 401(k) account. The repayment plan is very strict, and if you violate the repayment plan, then the 401(k) rep converts your loan into a withdrawal and takes out five $100s from your account and flushes them down the IRS toilet for you. She then sends you a nice note telling you what she did and never bothers you again. Oh yeah, if you quit or get fired you have to pay back your loan within 30 days. I don't need to remind you that coming up with $1000 or so at the same time as when you find out you are out of a job is not something most people want to do.

Your next option is the awful credit cards. They'll charge somewhere between 1.5% and 2.5% interest per month. So as long as you are not paying off your credit card balance, count on making a monthly trip to a trash basket labeled "credit card interest" and tossing a crisp $20 in for every thousand dollars you borrowed. Bye bye Jackson.

My point with these stories is that you have no good option, but you still have to get the money. You need the car to work, you need your health to live, and you don't want your mom to disown you. What you need to do is right now imagine someone in that situation and walk through the scenarios available to you; and then feel bad for that poor schmuck. Then slap yourself in the face and say "That could be me if I don't do something to prevent that from happening.

The something you need to do is create another bill for yourself called "unexpected". That bill should be about 5% to 10% of your take home pay. So if you make $1000 / week and take home about $750, your "unexpected should be $40 to $75 a week. Deposit it into a savings account every week, and don't touch it unless you have an unexpected and necessary expense. Remember: you don't want to be the poor schmuck throwing good money in the IRS toilet or credit card interest trash can.

When you ever get to $15,000 or so (some people never do), you have a decent enough safety net and you can start investing. That's for another chapter.

Chapter 8 -- Lifestyle Inequality Among Friends

The original title for this chapter was going to be "Income Inequality Among Friends". Income differential between friends is irrelevant if you live similar lifestyles. After thinking about the content of this chapter, the topic that really needs addressing is "Lifestyle Inequality Among Friends". As we move through life sometimes our spending patterns begin to fall out of alignment with friends. You may have a friend who buys a new car while you are still driving your old car. Or a friend that tries to convince you to spend $400 that you don't really feel you can justify buying front row tickets to a concert.

You don't have to justify your spending decisions to your friends. Just spend money on what you feel comfortable with spending it on. You'll find that some friends have the same interests as you and feel comfortable with spending money on the same things as you, and you'll identify incompatibilities with others. Then an interesting thing will happen. The whole issue will kind of disappear. You'll have a set of activities that you like to do and a set of friends that are interested in doing those things with you. Some of them will have higher or lower incomes than you, but it just won't matter, because you will all be doing what you like doing and spending the money you are comfortable with spending.

Another interesting thing will happen too. Savers will end up "self sorting" with other savers and people who earn less than themselves. Spenders will end up with people with higher incomes and other spenders. This self sorting mechanism is a virtuous cycle for savers. The more people stick to a savings ethic, the more able you are to stay away from the "keeping up with the Joneses" culture that we have now. Savers eventually forget what it's like to have a $150 dinner for two or to own a new luxury car or to play a round of golf at a private golf club with a $300 greens fee. They'll forget because none of their friends want to do these things or have ever done these things. They won't even hear people talk about those experiences. There is no opportunity to succumb to the temptation because it's just not part of the conversation.

As a matter of fact, in my experience, hanging around savers inspires people to save more. There are several personal finance gurus who have made a culture and community around the pride of saving money. Dave Ramsey comes to mind as a radio personality that does this. Mr. Money Moustache is a web personality that does this. In these communities spending lavishly is an item of shame and controlling expenses is a badge of honor. The best thing you can do with your social life to set yourself down the road to financial independence is to select friends with a strong savings ethic. Don't bother to try to keep up with the Joneses. Don't even bother trying to keep up with your friends who are trying to keep up with the Joneses.

Once your social life has sorted you into the group with similar financial habits, everything else just falls into place. You don't even have to try to save any more. Your lifestyle will just naturally lead to that result. Over time you'll get more invites to a hike on a nature trail (free) than a round of golf at the private club ($300). Even if you accept those invites with equal frequency, you'll be spending a lot less money on entertainment than you otherwise would. You'll feel a lot more comfortable with your decision to keep your eight year old Honda as you drive it to the hiking trail than if you have to valet it at the club. I personally feel uncomfortable whenever I hand my car keys to a valet who drives a car nicer than mine. On the other hand, at least I can be comfortable that he's not going to steal it.

So the thing to be concerned about in your circle of friends is not income inequality, it is lifestyle inequality. Pick friends who spend like you want to spend. You'll reduce the stress in your life and increase your wealth in the process. It's not hard. I'll be your friend. Join the community at TypeZFinance.com.

Chapter 9 -- Negotiating and How it Relates to Money

Negotiating is a double edged sword. On the one hand it is an obvious driver to improving the financial outcome of a transaction. On the other hand it can be time consuming, feel confrontational, and be unpleasant. So when should you choose to embark down the path of negotiation? If you've read this far you already know that my fall back course of action for anything that touches my finances is a cost benefit analysis.

The costs to negotiation are 1) the time it takes to go through the negotiation; 2) the possible damage to your long term relationship with the person you are negotiating with; 3) the personal discomfort you may feel with negotiating in this situation.

The benefit is straightforward - an improved price after you are done (maybe).

So obviously, all things being equal, you should negotiate more often, spend more time, and accept a higher risk of failure in negotiating higher cost items-- a house, a car, your rent, major home repair, a wedding, your salary, etc. All of these items have a fairly high cost. A 10% improvement in price will give you thousands of dollars - potentially a few months of take home pay. Absolutely it is imperative that you negotiate these items if you have any reasonable shot at improving your price.

Take the rent on an apartment as an example. Let's say your monthly rent is $1,500 and it is up for renewal next month. That's an $18K annual cost to you. If your negotiating efforts can lead to a rent 10% lower than it otherwise would be, that's $1,800 in your pocket, tax free. For most renters that's 2 or 3 week's wages. That's a vacation. You better believe that it is worth it to spend some time talking with your landlord and making an effort to lower your rent.

Sometimes when I encourage friends to negotiate the big ticket items in their lives, I get a response like "I don't want to rock the boat..." or "I don't want to do anything to lose this deal..." Both of those statements suggest that my friends believe that whoever they are negotiating with doesn't care at all about coming to an agreement with you. That couldn't be further from the truth. If your negotiating partner didn't care, they wouldn't make a reasonable offer to begin with. And they might not even make an offer at all.

Let's go back to the apartment example. If your landlord offers you a renewal, it means he wants you there! If he didn't want you to renew, he wouldn't offer the renewal. Remember that. Next, I know I'm stating the obvious but, your landlord is a person too. Your landlord may also be thinking "I don't want to rock the boat..." or "I don't want to do anything to lose this deal..." Your landlord might be just as eager to keep you in your apartment as you are to stay. But you'll never find out if you don't open up the negotiation. So go for it.

If you begin a negotiation process with your landlord and give him every signal you are willing to spend a lot of time negotiating, your landlord may decide that the negotiation isn't worth his time. He may just give in right away and you won't even have to spend the time negotiating in the first place. What a win / win for you.

Your landlord may also react in exactly the opposite manner. Your landlord may decide the negotiation is not worth it and decide not to negotiate at all. "Take it or leave it," he says. That's not a loss for you either. Give in. You still got your apartment. The point here is that opening up the negotiation in a friendly way has no downside and potential upside. Don't take it personally at all. Some people get so attached to "winning" a negotiation that they lose sight of what they really want. In this example you really want the apartment at the best possible deal. Giving in accomplishes that goal.

Often I see people choosing not to negotiate in a situation like the apartment example above, but they'll spend an hour negotiating with a stranger from Craigslist over $100 concert tickets. Their potential gain for their efforts might be $10. It's not usually worth an hour of your time especially when the gain is far from certain. The most a person should spend negotiating a $100 item is five minutes or so. If your negotiating partner starts down the road of negotiating and you sense it's going to last more than five minutes. Give in or walk away. Don't bother engaging any further on the issue. My advice is the same to both buyers and sellers. It's not worth it.

Another example- You want to buy a washing machine valued around $500. It's not worth it to spend all day comparison shopping to save maybe $50 since it's probably going to cost you an hour for each store you drive to and visit. Pick the store you like best and go there and pick the best one. Spend at most 15 or 20 minutes negotiating with the salesperson if you think it may help.

So my point with this chapter is that you should decide to negotiate your purchases on a case by case basis. Sometimes it is crucial to negotiate, other times it is pointless. This chapter helps you know the difference.

Chapter 10 -- Interest Rates

This book is designed to help you in the real world so I'll avoid all textbook definitions and formulas. When you are considering borrowing money, interest rates don't matter unless you are borrowing money for an investment. Your out of pocket costs are what counts for consumer borrowing. Whenever you are thinking of buying something, the seller wants to make it as easy as possible for you to buy. Sellers often offer financing and disguise the true cost of your purchase by charging financing fees in addition to interest. So, for a non investment purchase, you must compare the cash price of your purchase to the "all in" cost if you finance.

The "all in" cost is your payment amount times the number of payments plus your initial financing fees, plus any other required purchases plus any late fees and other nonsense the finance company can manage to add to your total cost. Look at that "all in" cost. Now compare that cost to the item that you want. Is your potential purchase worth that all in cost? If not, walk away. It's that simple.

For example, if you plan on financing your car[3], then you have to ignore the sale price. That's the price

---

3 I hope not. I devoted all of Chapter 6 to discussing the stupidity of getting a car loan. However, I know some of you have "a friend" who has a car loan. This example is for their benefit.

offered to people paying cash. You aren't one of those people. If the sale price for your car is $25,000, the financing department may offer to finance your car for $400 per month for 72 months (6 years). In addition, you will have to pay an application fee, and origination fee of $150 each. Finally, your dealer may require you to purchase a maintenance plan costing $500 per year. Your cost for the car is $400 x 72 + $150 + $150 +$500 x 6 = $32,100. If that car that other people are buying for $25,000 isn't worth $32,100 to you, then walk away.

Now you may decide that you will pay cash... by charging the purchase to your credit card. That's funny logic to me, but I'll go with it. Your "all in" cost includes all of the interest and late charges you are going to pay between now and the time you plan to pay off your credit card bill. If you can't foresee the day when your credit card bill will be paid off, then you are not buying the item at all, and your cost for this item is equal to the interest charge times the number of months you have left to live. A $100 item charged to a credit card will cost you $2 a month, forever. If you are young and have 50 years or so (600 months) left to live then you'll be paying $1200 for that $100 item. Unless it's food and you are starving, it's probably not worth it.

You can use the same sort of logic with interest rates when you are saving money. Interest rates are horribly low right now. Even the highest interest online savings accounts pay only 1% annual interest right now (2016). So your $1000 savings account will earn you only $10 if you keep your money in for a whole year. "Why even bother... said the man with no money."

Before anyone starts complaining about a savings account than has $1010 next year, I want to invite them to do a little thought experiment. Imagine taking your $1000 and converting it into cash-- 10 crisp $100 bills. Lay them out side by side on your kitchen table, and then do whatever you want with them. Now ask yourself how much of that money do you have left in one year's time. If you're honest, the number is probably zero. You probably won't be able to resist the temptation to spend that cash you are looking at.

So, even at 1% interest, savings accounts are still a great deal. Go online and pick the highest interest rate savings account you can find and open an account there. Don't spend too much time on the process, though. Improving your interest rate by 0.1% is only worth $1 per year per $1000 in your savings account. To me, a dollar in additional taxable income is worth only about a minute of my personal time. If you have $10K or $100K to save, it might be worth using a full lunch break to find the highest interest account available. Finding a good savings account is not rocket science. Higher interest is better than lower interest. As long as interest rates are higher than zero, you're making a good move by opening the account. Of course make sure there are no monthly fees associated with your account.

Chapter 11 -- Budgeting

To me writing about budgeting is like writing about dieting. If I had to write a diet book it would be four words long-- "Eat Less. Exercise More." Simple advice, and guaranteed results.

My budgeting book would be almost as simple. It would be five words instead of four-- "Spend Less than You Earn". So often personal finance experts who write about budgeting make it seem like budgeting is far more complicated than it needs to be. Here's why they do that. First, it's hard to become a well respected expert if all of your expert advice on a topic can fit in a tweet. It would also be very hard to sell books if your book is only five words long.

Another reason is a bit less obvious. There's high demand to make budgeting seem complex. After all millions of people are buying books describing overly complicated Rube Goldberg like systems for budgeting that take hundreds of pages to explain. I've thought about the cause for over twenty years and believe I have uncovered the answer. Some people who have not been successful at the budgeting process have a need to make it seem complex. Those people do not want to admit to themselves that they have not yet devoted the discipline to succeed at something so simple, yet so important.

I want to speak to those people that are not yet budgeting in their personal lives. First, the fact that you have not yet budgeted doesn't mean you can't budget or you will never budget. Second, you don't need a 200 page personal finance book on budgeting and the "envelope system" to budget. As a matter of fact, for you, seeking a book like that would be counterproductive. If you haven't successfully gone down the one step process of spending less than you earn, then there is no reason to think you would be more successful at a budgeting process that takes 200 pages to explain. Avoid the temptation to make budgeting more complicated than you know it is. You can decide to begin budgeting in your finances today. You don't need any books, education, special equipment, or particular skills. All you need is a determination to start right now.

Getting control of your finances is definitely reward enough for your budgeting efforts. However people who are budgeting and adhering to my five word budgeting guide get an additional reward. They don't worry about their finances any more.

People who are conservative with their budgets don't worry about their finances. Instead, they think about their finances. They think thoughts like "If I increase saving by $500 per month, I'll be able to retire at 55 instead of 60..." That's not really a worrisome thought, that's more of a motivating thought.

Or maybe "If I get fired today, I have enough money to support myself for six months..." Again, that's not a worrisome thought, more of a comforting thought.

Or possibly "Based on my current income and expenses, I can afford a $250,000 house. Once I get enough for a down payment, I'll be able to afford a $300K house."

People who are conservative with their budgets think about their finances a lot. It is motivating to them and helps them stay on track. I have also found that people who think about their finances a lot become very good at ball park estimating some complicated personal finance questions (like "How much do I need to save per month to retire in 10 years..."). They become good at it because they spend a lot of time thinking about these issues.

I personally find that I think about my long term financial picture while I am running, especially when I was training for a marathon a few years ago. I would have an hour or more with just my thoughts. Thinking about and solving personal finance questions just came naturally while I was running along. It was a good use of my mental time and a good distracter when I was physically exhausted.

Some people say budgeting involves allocating a certain number of dollars to five, ten, or maybe even twenty expense categories and then diligently logging each expenditure into one of those categories. That's

46

complicated and unnecessary for an individual's finances. There's one and only one budget category-- spending. And it's quite simple to come up with a budget limit-- less than you earn.

Over time you might decide that you want to come up with a more intricate way to estimate future expenses and I'll talk about that in a later chapter. More detailed budgets are not necessary if you don't want to. Get started today.

Chapter 12 -- Conclusion

This book, <u>Starting to Make Money</u> is the second in my five part series on personal finance. The goal of this book is to get you thinking about everyday money issues that everyone faces. You learned about car loans, everyday spending and saving decisions and money issues affecting your social life. This book takes the personal finance foundation developed in Book one and applies it to the real world. After reading this book you are comfortable effectively managing your personal budget. You are generating positive cash flow in your life and are starting down a path that will lead to traditional investing and wealth building. Continue your journey through all five books and you'll be certain to **Never Make an Uninformed Financial Decision Again**.

Book one is titled <u>Understanding Money</u>. The goal of this book is to begin to get you thinking about your attitudes and beliefs regarding the basics of personal finance: Money, earning, spending, saving, and investing. In thinking about these topics, you will begin to understand how your beliefs shape your financial behaviors for better or worse. This book is the foundation for all the information and discussion contained in the remaining four books on personal finance topics that you are almost sure to face in your life.

The third book is titled <u>An Adult Relationship with Money</u>. The topics in this book are where most personal finance books start. To me, starting with this book is kind of like starting to build a house on the third floor, or teaching algebra before multiplication. There's no way you can be successful in managing your taxes, investments, loans, and financial coaches until you have the foundation contained in the first two books. This is the book most similar to traditional personal finance books. You'll understand this book more though, because the topics in the first two books give you the foundation of financial knowledge necessary to understand personal finance. The knowledge you gather in this book will likely guide you to financial decisions in the near future that improve your finances by a few thousand dollars over the poor financial decisions you might have made without this book.

The fourth book is titled <u>Now You Have Money</u>. This book discusses financial issues and decisions you'll face if you follow the guidance in the first three books. It discusses retirement investing, annuities, and other issues related to managing a six or seven figure net worth. If you're not in that wealth category yet, you will be soon enough. Just follow the guidance from the first three books. It's great to be ahead of the game and have the peace of mind knowing how to handle your future wealth before you actually have it.

The fifth and final book is titled <u>Extra Credit - Money for Fun</u>. This book is the final step of the personal finance journey. Among other things, it discusses the personal finance issues around being set for life and keeping yourself educated about personal finance. If you're not set for life yet, don't fret. Just follow the guidance in the first four books and be patient. You'll make it. Think of this book as the "continuing ed" book on personal finance.

I welcome all feedback. Feel free to contact me at Hayden@ForwardFinancialPlanners.com. This is your gateway to share one-off commentary, suggestions for future books, or to get on the distribution list for updates related to future publications.

You can also subscribe to www.TypeZFinance.com for my weekly thoughts on personal finance issues that have caught my attention.

www.ingramcontent.com/pod-product-compliance
Lightning Source LLC
Chambersburg PA
CBHW071824170526
45167CB00003B/1409